CENSORING THE CENSORS

By Steve Beai

CHICAGO SPECTRUM PRESS
LOUISVILLE, KENTUCKY 40207

Chicago Spectrum Press
4848 Brownsboro Center
Louisville, KY 40207
1-800-594-5190

Printed in the U.S.A.

10 9 8 7 6 5 4 3 2 1

Library of Congress Number:
ISBN: 1-886094-81-0

You gave me the love of words and music, more, you gave of yourself and always believed.

Until we meet again, you are with me always.

For Deno Libei

Acknowledgments

Many people were instrumental in bringing this compilation to life, most notably, in complete nonsensical disorder, the following: Frank and Paulette for the life, Mike Olson for the laughs, Harlan Ellison for his words that inspired me to stand, Michelle Walker for the love, Kylee Walker for the innocence, Dr. John Worley for the eternal friendship, Don Eime, Bob Crouch, Terri Worley, Dorothy Kavka and the good folks at Evanston Publishing, John B. Rosenman for trust and the chance of a lifetime, Jeannette Hopper and the 1990 Executive Board of SPWAO and the assholes who, by their actions of bans, boycotts and bullying, insure that the most offensive expressions of human creativity get the most exposure possible.

TABLE OF CONTENTS

FOREWORD
Censoring the Censors Revisited

When I became editor of the SPWAO Newsletter in January, 1989, I received a huge care package of submissions on file from P.S. Weber, the previous editor. After tiptoeing around this daunting and ominous legacy for a few minutes, I finally girded up my loins and broke its massive seals. Then I took a deep breath and plunged inside the voluminous contents, looking for something that would spark interest.

Right away, I got lucky.

The item I ran across, kneeling there in my den on that cold January afternoon, was Steve Beai's virgin voyage on choppy censorial seas. A quick scan produced a loud "Hot damn!", for such an item was exactly what I wanted. I found the article well written, stirringly controversial, and above all, of potential interest to all member writers and artists, for it dealt with and explored the complex threats to free creative expression which exist in America. I fired off a letter to Steve almost immediately, asking him if he'd consider doing a regular column. He said yes, and Censoring the Censors was born.

Rereading these columns (and the sometimes vituperative letters they inspired) has given me great pleasure, and I think they will also for those of you who find them here for the first time. In his very first column for the March/April 1989 issue, Steve called censorship "an intellectual cancer", and for the next two years, he wielded a keen verbal scalpel in his efforts to carve it out and warn others about its dangers. During these years, Steve took on a veritable Who's Who of Censors, including "President Wildmon and Vice-President Helms", Tipper "I Love Rock and Roll" Gore, and the various forces that sought to keep us from either reading or seeing "The Last Temptation of Christ". For good measure he also included such controversial subjects as Andrew Dice Clay, 2 Live Crew, the FCC, the Mapplethorpe case and the National Endowment for the Arts, Satanism, Heavy Metal music, and too many others to mention.

It probably won't surprise you as you read these columns that not everyone liked what Steve wrote or wanted to take him home. He did, after all, take very firm stands which ruffled more than a few feathers. Some members felt he was opinionated, even prejudiced. Some didn't like his use of words like "shit" and "crap" and "pissed off" and wanted me to delete such expletives. But I'll remind them that Steve clearly stated back in the July/Aug 1989 issue, exactly what his game plan would be. He wrote, "Keep in mind that if you hate what I have to say, I may very well pick apart your written missive without mercy. (Isn't freedom great?)"

The issue, as I see it, remains now what it was then: freedom of choice and expression. Such freedom, I believe, is so precious and important that it is better to be too vigorous and irreverent and yes, even offensive in its defense than too little. Better to rub a few feathers the wrong way and put a few noses out of joint than to pull your punches and observe pitty-pat rules of etiquette. As Steve so often pointed out in his columns, those who set themselves up as moral arbiters and feel they have the God-given right to decide what you and I can and cannot see/read/listen to, etc. in the privacy of our own homes often have no compunction whatsoever about how far they will go to serve their cause. They'll use terrorist tactics, cost you your job or business, and throw you in jail for exercising your First

Amendment rights. And sometimes, not often, but often enough, they'll outright kill you.

These, then, are two years of Steve Beai's Censoring the Censors, and I believe they represent the SPWAO Newsletter at its best. They were so good, in fact, that just before the end of my second year as editor, they caused a well-known small-press publisher and editor to write me and ask if he could do a similar column in rebuttal to Steve's views! That might have been interesting and lively indeed, for it would have opened up an unprecedented forum for both sides. But by that time, both Steve and I had other projects and felt it was time to move on.

In closing, I'd like to thank Steve for contributing so richly to our organization's pages, and especially for never ever taking offense at the letters I published in return which bitterly attacked him. He could have, you know. It's human nature. But I know that he always believed that the other guy deserved his shot too, whether he was right or wrong, in the interest of freedom.

–John B. Rosenman

INTRODUCTION:
The First Essay, August 1988

I first became conscious to the threat of censorship in the Spring of 1988. Having never viewed myself as one who champions causes, I was quite surprised by my newfound awareness. Watching in an almost mystical awe, Martin Scorsese, George Romero, Harper Lee, Stephen King, Norman Mailer, along with Maurice Sendak, Walt Disney and Warner Brothers come under attack by special interest groups who wanted not only to remove the offending items from public access, but who also hoped to ultimately close down a host of supporting retailers through bans, boycotts and book burnings.

I thought that was wrong.

And *that* was my entire opinion on the subject.

So I sat down and wrote *The Last Temptation and The Day After*, secure in the knowledge that the essay was cathartic at best, but would probably never be published. However, without regard to the fact that this essay talked plenty about *The Last Temptation of Christ*, but failed to mention a thing about the made-for-TV Nuclear-Bomb-Hits-Kansas City movie *The Day After*, I submitted it to the Small Press Writer's and Artist's Organization, of which I had recently become a member. That was August of 1988.

Six months later, I received a letter from John Rosenman, praising the article. He suggested a regular column and I said, "Yeah, sure, OK". Then I turned cartwheels for a couple of hours. Then I wondered what else I would say. At this point in my career, my medium was the world of make-believe and dark fantasies. I had never written down a word of non-fiction on the installment plan for an Editor. After the initial shock and the fabulous fun-filled rollercoaster ride through the mountains of self-doubt, I wrote the first column.

But I'm getting ahead of myself.

Little did I know when I accepted John's offer, that the simplistic, juvenile opinion I had formed would grow into the personal and professional philosophy on the issue that I have today.

The following essay rings a bit hollow, at best. However, it was the jumping-off point of an evolving idea that would lead me to examine myself as well as the world around me. It is presented here for the first time.

THE FIRST ESSAY
The Last Temptation and the Day After
August 1988

To most writers, hearing the word "censorship" strikes a special chord of fear in the mind. If it doesn't, then the writer in question is a craftsman of "safe" prose or poetry and has nothing to fear from the hordes of glassy-eyed people who seek to be their brother's keeper. Or so he or she may think.

The latest furor that has the censors, coming to us in the form of "Christians", in a tizzy, is the soon-to-be-released film by Martin Scorsese, *The Last Temptation of Christ*. Waging a particularly valiant effort to erase Freedom of Choice from future history is Donald E. Wildmon, along with religious leaders throughout the U.S. Apparently, Mr. Wildmon was involved in pre-release screenings of the film and didn't like what he saw. In the interest of space, I will not attempt to synopsize the movie from the article I received from Mount Calvary Lutheran Church in Fullerton, Nebraska, but I will be more than happy to provide copies of the article to interested parties who include a SASE along with their request. To tell you the truth, the movie sounds pretty funny. I probably won't go see it, but I may change my mind so it would be nice to have the opportunity. And that, my friends, is what it's all about.

The Last Temptation of Christ is said to be an outrage, offensive to anyone with a modicum of decency. Call me a pervert if you will, but I'd like to make up my own mind. That's what it's *really* about. Individual choice to plunk down a few bucks to see a movie, or buy a book, and enjoy it or hate it. Choice.

The last time censorship flexed its muscle was too close to home for me. Four blocks away from where I live sits my old high school, Park Hill. *One* family effectively protested Harper Lee's outstanding novel *To Kill A Mockingbird* from being taught at Park Hill Senior High School. Ten years earlier, I had the good fortune to read that book in a literature class at the very same school. *To Kill A Mockingbird* was banned from not only the class, but from the school library, and remains absent to this day. I include this example for those of us who have yet to write screenplays directed by Martin Scorsese.

The fact is, any and all of us may be next in line to defend our rights to write, direct, publish and dream in our individual styles. More and more, it looks as though we may lose the battle to those who would place themselves in a position to decide for the rest of us what is good and bad, what we don't ever need to see or read or think.

The Last Temptation article urged boycott of not only the movie, but every business of which MCA is the parent company, closing with the address of MCA. It is printed here now, in the interest of equal time.

Chairman Tom Pollock
MCA, Inc.
100 Universal City Plaza
Universal City, CA 91608

The article also included Mr. Pollock's office phone number, so: (818) 777-1000.

Although I would hesitate to call, I'm sure Mr. Pollock wouldn't mind running across a friendly letter of support in the mailbags full of hate mail.

Although I do not consider myself a champion of causes, as a writer, this is one I simply cannot overlook. I urge my fellow members to get involved, in whatever way possible. The next book or movie you save could be your own.

In closing, I would like to leave you with some words spoken by Spencer Tracy from Stanley Kramer's 1960 production of *Inherit the Wind*, a movie that fought its own battle with the censors 28 years ago. If you haven't seen it, it's still around. Check it out.

"And soon...with banners flying and drums beating, we'll be marching backward — *backward*! Through the glorious age of that sixteenth century when bigots burned a man who dared bring enlightenment and intelligence to the human mind..."

INTRODUCTION: Column One, March/April 1989

I had decided to treat this column as *Cliff Notes* from a teacher to his students. That idea remained for the entire project, but I decided to drop the "Hard Lessons" prefix in favor of the succinct title "Censoring the Censors" after this installment.

Without realizing it, I was opening the floodgates for both opposition and acceptance on a scale I could not imagine. When I was contacted by John via a brief letter that said, in essence, that the column was a grand creation, but that I shouldn't "pull any punches," I resolved to speak from the deepest (and sometimes blackest) regions of my heart as passionately as I was able to in my individual voice.

This column spoke of what I knew — fiction — and played upon the minds of all members who were left guessing right up to the closing word. Looking back, it was probably the only column that generated a chuckle from readers.

COLUMN ONE HARD LESSONS: CENSORING THE CENSORS

March/April 1989

There is a certain word that I use in my fiction that my wife is not particularly fond of. Most of the time I'm not even aware that I'm using *The Word*. However, when I present my wife with a new piece of prose to proofread (say that three times fast), I can always tell by a loud groan coming from the other room that I've used *The Word*. Now, I always defend to the death my right to use *The Word*, but one time I went too far. After hearing a cacophony of groans, I rushed out of the office, immediately blurting out the following:

"What? What? Funny? Sad? Scary? *What*?"

My wife stood up and threw the manuscript to the coffee table. She looked like a Japanese monster, nostrils flaring, radioactive steam pouring from her mouth. "You used *The Word*," she said. "*Four* times."

So, being the soft-spoken soul that I am, I walked briskly to the table, rescued my manuscript, and looked her straight in the eye before making a bigger mistake than using *The Word*. I said: "Fine. You can forget reading another goddamn thing I write." *That* took the wind out of her sails pretty quick. Proud of myself, I headed back to my office.

Which brings me to the Hard Lessons of this article, as promised. No, my wife didn't divorce me. But I had done something contrary to what I consider a basic philosophy. But you're not going to get off the hook with a simple explanation. Instead, here's another example, one that will further your steps to a lucid understanding of the latter example.

In the February 20 issue of *U.S. News & World Report*, the letters column received a half-dozen responses centering around religious broadcaster James Dobson's interview with Theodore Bundy. You remember him, Ol' Ted. He's the serial killer they had to carry to the electric chair a few weeks back. To recap briefly for those of you who may have missed this interview, Ted Bundy refused an interview with everyone except for Mr. Dobson, who has battled the scourge of pornography since he started his career. And Mr. Bundy, having nothing to lose, blamed his adventures strangling women on — you guessed it — pornography. So now we come to the response from an article in the February 6 issue of *U.S. News*. One such letter came from Edith Ellenbogen of Merrick, NY. She wrote a very nice letter disagreeing with the media coverage of the notorious Mr. Bundy in general, and then...she flushed her noble stance right down the toilet by writing, in part, "...we will boycott any such programs and their sponsors...if we get them where it hurts, namely, network ratings and pocketbooks, perhaps we will be able to bring the words *good taste* into the TV vocabulary."

Ah, the Hard Lesson.

Collectively, we, as creative artists, should never stop the fight against censorship. To create a work that expresses oneself is as basic to us as eating and, fellow members, the sad fact is that we are in more danger than ever before of losing our right to satisfy this basic need. I have picketed the picketers outside of a run-down theatre in Kansas — the only theatre dashing enough to show *The Last Temptation of Christ*, while multi-cinemas such as AMC and Dickinson balked. I have written letter after letter to the school board of Park Hill R-5 district after hearing that Harper Lee's fine novel *To Kill A Mockingbird* was banned from the school library as well as classes at Park Hill

Senior High School (where I graduated) by a black family who, after taking time *not* to read the book considered it racist. Yes, I said a black family. Currently, I am launching a one-man campaign of letters against Waldenbooks, B. Dalton Bookseller, and Barnes and Noble for not carrying *The Satanic Verses* by Salman Rushdie, a book I have a desire to read that these stores are not carrying because of maniacal death threats from the glorious nation of Insane Islam against Rushdie *and* his publisher, Viking Penguin. Note that my efforts have consisted of letters and picketing and a few lines ago, I said we should never stop our fight against censorship.

I did not say, however, stop at nothing. Censorship is an intellectual cancer and like all forms of cancer, it has a tendency to grow, to infest the very cells which fight against it. When Alexandria, VA artist Alice Sims lost custody of her children for twenty-four hours because some geek in a photo lab thought the prints of her painting "Water Babies" in which she used her children as models constituted child pornography, she did not launch even a letter-writing campaign, and she most certainly did not ban commercial photo labs or their parent companies. Likewise, I still shop at Waldenbooks and still believe in the inherent integrity of the Park Hill school system. Still, our voices are heard and if enough of us care to join the battle and keep our wits about us, we can effectively stem the rising tide of censors, whether they be Bible-thumping fanatics condemning a movie, or zealots condemning not only a book, but a man's life. Because, water babies, these people are doing what they set out to do. They're destroying freedom of choice and, in the process, they're destroying freedom of creativity. One of our works may very well be next if we remain silent, or become as they are; fighting boycotts with more boycotts, censoring thoughts against thoughts. It doesn't take long to write a letter of concern or hold a picket sign that says "Thank God I am Free To See This Movie."

My wife still reads every story I write. She still hates *The Word*, and I still disagree, but we respect each other's right to do so. Oh, yes — the word?

Girl.

INTRODUCTION:
Column Two, May/June 1989

The research involved in preparing this next column unearthed some surprising information. Prior to my discovery, I had thought that censorship was an activity engaged in by fanatics hiding behind religion, politics, and other twisted factions of our society. Being so naive, I never once thought that censorship dribbled and seeped into the world of high finance as a tool used for making a buck.

I was also surprised at the influx of mail I began to receive in response to the first column, blissfully unaware of the fact that it was all positive. Because, you see, so far I had said nothing *wrong*, nothing to rock the sensibilities of those readers who agreed with the spirit of what I wrote. I was still pulling my punches somewhat, waiting for John Rosenman's confirmation letter in order to feel him out as best as I could.

That was all about to change.

COLUMN TWO
May/June 1989

First off, I'd like to thank those people who wrote to me offering copies of *The Satanic Verses*. I am happy to report that I walked into Waldenbooks at Metro North Mall in Kansas City and was able to purchase my own copy from one of a dozen displays in that store. I also must commend Melinda Jaeb for the back cover of *Witness To The Bizarre* #3. Nice going, Ms. Jaeb. For those of you who have not secured a subscription to *WTTB*, I urge you to do so. Now, on to my tirade.

I had the extreme displeasure of watching *Aliens* on my local network affiliate a few weeks ago. Although I own a copy of the original theatrical release, which runs well over two hours, I thought it might be fun to see how television would handle a few of my favorite scenes in the movie; namely, the action scenes. So, instead of popping my videotape into the VCR, I turned on and, later, tuned out, the television. After viewing less than two hours of a 160-minute movie and more than 20 minutes of commercials, a soft-spoken fellow may have simply said "*Oops*".

I was so pissed off I damn near blew the television to pieces. I would've too, but before I could load the shotgun, my wife gently reminded me that the cat was sitting on top of the Groove Tube. Besides, our Sony stereo is right next to the TV and I probably would've killed it as well, which would have been a tragic loss, since I listen to music a hell of a lot more than I watch TV — I have a broader range of choice as far as the stereo goes, even though the FCC is managing to slowly gain a stranglehold on that tiny, insignificant freedom as well. But I'll talk about that next time.

For now, let's talk TV.

As I suffered through the deli-version of *Aliens*, I also suffered through a series of commercials telling me how I can get my laundry whiter and brighter, as well as why I'm a stupid sonofabitch if I don't rush right out and buy a new Ford Escort that gets great mileage, coupled with no power, that I will have to replace a month before I pay it off. But — and now we get down to the real juicy stuff — I had the privilege of watching a half-dozen couples stick their tongues between each other's lips while a voice-over announcer asked me "*Want love?*" And then answered their own question by telling me to "*Get Close-Up*". Of course, all of this lip-sucking was presented in close-up shots, and of course, the commercial was for Close-Up toothpaste. Meanwhile, the scenes of Ripley squashing an alien while driving a futuristic getaway car, Bishop, the "synthetic person", getting torn apart by the Queen alien, and many more scenes too painful to recount, were cut from the movie.

We pause for a commercial break.

The "Big Three", CBS, ABC and NBC, vie for the right to air a top box-office release, between three and five years after the theatrical debut. Once a network secures this film, it would be easy enough to present it uncut and uncensored — you know — just like cable television.

But something happens from acquisition of the film to the time you get to see it, and it's not what you think. To really believe that one of the "Big Three" is genuinely concerned about the effect on the public if they air a scene with Ripley squashing a giant insect is horseshit. That *Close-Up* commercial was ten times as strong, no doubt giving thousands of SF boys and girls raging hard-ons and hot flashes because that's exactly what it was supposed to do. No modesty on the Censor's part there, because, you see, commercial television is not genuinely concerned about negative effects on *you* as an individual — if a little off-color material is presented to push a product, that's okay. They're concerned with negative effects on you as a *consumer*. The fact is, that the sponsors, the commercial giants, have their own little board of censors and *they* decide what you see and don't see. Naturally, they're not called Censors, they may be called a Board of Trustees, or a Program Director, or an Ad Exec. But if they hear alarm bells in their heads, then they won't put their commercials on during the running of the movie, and the network is not in a position to deny any sponsor due to the costs in presenting a movie, so they take the heat where cutting scenes is concerned. Keep in mind that every faction involved needs to make a substantial profit. In an industry that relies upon thousand-dollar seconds and multi-million-dollar deals to procure top movies, every commercial counts. Hypothetically speaking, if the Powers-That-Be employed by *Close-Up* toothpaste decides that a certain scene in a certain movie will overpower the effect of their commercial, they will negotiate to cut that scene. And they will win, because — right. Glad to see you're catching on.

And now back to our feature presentation.

So, what is the solution to this covert form of censorship, a daily occurrence that is hard to spot, yet ever present? Well, if we were one of the censors, we would immediately demand a boycott of the products offered in the commercials and a boycott of the networks offering the truncated films to the public for the benefit of the commercial sponsors.

But we're not censors, are we? We won't commit a second wrong to make a right, because that's poor math — one plus one equals two. Don't misunderstand me — I *liked* the Close-Up commercial. But not at the expense of a movie I tuned in to watch, cut to ribbons for reasons that make me want to blow puke all over the carpet.

Now, you might think I'm picking on a specific commercial, but it's not as simple as that. The commercial *is* strong, it's had me thinking about Close-Up toothpaste for weeks, not necessarily because I saw it four or five times during the network presentation of *Aliens* either. I'm a big fan of Warner Bros. cartoons, I watch them every Saturday morning from 9 a.m. to 10 a.m., and guess what commercial I see twice in that hour? But, you may be asking, how does that relate? Babies, I'll tell you. All over the country, Warner Bros. cartoons are being pulled from stations due to the implied violence present in the animation, specifically, *The Road Runner*.

It's a tough and very ambiguous fight and sometimes it's easy to let the censors get out of control because we can't see it happening, or we don't think it's *that* bad, or we simply do not know what to do. In the humble opinion of the censors, something is wrong. That's okay with us, right?

Right. Everyone is entitled to his or her opinion.

But it's being taken too far. It's coming down to a question of control over every channel we have access to. A small number of people are deciding what's right and wrong based on *their* standards for the great majority of those who choose to remain silent because "things are going okay, why rock the boat? It's just TV". Of course, if a little off-color material is presented to push a product, well, that's okay, too. Right?

Wrong.

We have a secret solution. A secret solution that's available to everyone but the censors because, by virtue of their power, they haven't been able to figure it out.

Regardless of opinion, we can change the channel or turn the set off. For now, anyway. Maybe someday we won't even have that luxury.

Oops.

INTRODUCTION:
Column Three, July/August 1989

By this time, I was pulling no punches whatsoever, striking my keyboard with a vengeance. My personal beliefs began to take shape in the column's words and it became evident (to myself as well as the readers who responded) that I had loaded and let fly with both barrels. Music was my passion for this column and I attacked parents like a serial killer attacks hitchhikers. I also printed a quote from a letter by Doni Lazenby. (Doni would later take over the column after I became Treasurer of SPWAO and John Rosenman passed the torch as Editor, but by then, the organization had decided that it was better to kiss the membership's ass — whose total IQ I believe to this day does not break two digits — than to present anything that would remotely upset any retard who paid their 15 bucks in dues.)

Intoxicated by the rash of positive letters, I made a public appeal for more letters, adding a disclaimer for those who might want to write for calling me a worthless piece of human trash. By now, I was entrenched in the job like a fat tick, and knew that anyone who thought it might be neat to attack me would be painfully surprised at the verbal weapons their opponent had in his arsenal.

COLUMN THREE
July/August 1989

At 7:42 Central Standard Time on May 26, 1989, radio stations across the nation went silent for 30 seconds to remind listeners what life would be like without radio. If you were in your car, or cooking breakfast, or sitting at your job, you heard silence. Dead silence. On every station in the United States. Despite my attempts to discover the reason for this exercise, it remains a mystery. To me, anyway.

Whatever lesson the stations were trying to teach, the silence was by no means long enough. It should have been hours long, perhaps even a complete 24-hour silence. For those of you who missed this, it was kind of like the sound of one hand clapping.

I consider radio one of my most cherished means of entertainment and relaxation, from Public Radio right down to the heaviest heavy metal station. When I write, when I sit on the front porch, when I drive, I listen to Rock music, the louder the better. Where I live affords me this luxury of ear-splitting volume — I bother no one and no one bothers me. And the music doesn't end at Hard Rock — I have a CD and album collection as diverse as a music critic: Jazz, Blues, Rock, Punk Rock, a little country, classical, etc. I have spoken word albums, comedy albums, old-time radio shows — *ah, old-time radio shows.*

Now, I know what you're saying: "Wait a minute, Beai — we don't care about your music library — what does this mean?"

It means that it's time to get pissed.

Only the Shadow knows...heh, heh, heh...

The FCC has imposed substantial fines and, in some cases, completely shut down radio stations until they made a format change. The message here: Rock n' Roll kills and suggestive lyrics destroys the morals of this entire country. We've all heard about the extremely isolated cases where some teenage dipshit sat in his room for 72 hours ingesting inordinate amounts of acid and listening to Judas Priest and then went out and offed his parents and the family dog. Tragic, isn't it? Boy, I'd guess we'd better label those albums and firebomb them godless radio stations, right, Clem? *Yee-hah*!

Lamont Cranston is turning over in his grave.

What I want to know is where the hell those parents were all the while their kid was grilling his brain? It doesn't matter, you say? The parents aren't at fault, you say? The solution is putting a warning label on records? Great! Let's do it — after all, we already know what good such labels do on cigarettes, right? I'm looking at a pack of Marlboros next to my monitor, and I can tell you firsthand that the warning label sure makes me nervous. And when I'm nervous, I smoke. Likewise, putting labels on records. Man, I'll tell you what. If the next Van Halen album comes out and stirs up a lot of "concerned parents", you can bet your ass that I'll rush right out to the nearest record store, wait in line behind an army of kids, and buy it. If a radio station comes under fire for the material presented by the DJs because it's labeled "off-color" or "offensive", make no mistake that it's the station I'll be listening to, because that's where the action is, that's the station that will afford me the most entertainment. Pour some more sugar on the ground, honey, we need to get rid of all the ants.

I received a note from SPWAO member Doni Lazenby that I'd like to quote, in part: "*...censors, in effect, are trying to be everyone's parents...condemning those...trying to be parents of free choice...*" Well said, Ms. Lazenby. The fact is that we don't need more boycotts, bans, labels, legislature, and censorship. How about a stiff screening program for potential parents? You wanna take on the responsibility of having a kid, then, by God, take on the responsibility of raising it. Not good, huh? And why is that? Oh, because the decision to become a parent is based on — that's right — *individual, free choice*.

Dear readers, allow me to digress for a moment, if only for the purpose of making one minor point.

My parents, Frank and Paulette, stood by while their only son, yours truly, journeyed into the land of live music, playing the drums for a rock band at the tender age of eighteen. I traveled with the band, slept with the band, played in some real dive bars with the band and, ultimately, gave it up. Now I'm content to listen to the music and bash my drums alone in my office. My parents worried, don't get me wrong. They worried when I went out of town, worried when I watched horror movies and read Famous Monsters of Filmland magazine, worried about everything regarding my well-being. But, and here's where we separate the parents from the posers — they *knew* what I was doing, took an active interest in every crazy thing I valued. I can assure you that I had no secret sessions alone with Judas Priest and thoughts of murder. My parents knew all about that. They weren't afraid of sex education, they welcomed it, because they didn't want their son to become a father before he was able to handle fatherhood. (I'm still not able to handle fatherhood, but that's another story.)

Wow, all of this lunatic raving, the column's almost at an end, and I haven't even touched on the old-time radio shows, let alone how to deal with the present rash of censorship on radio. Let me take a deep breath, then I'll reload and let fly.

Thanks.

Surprisingly, every bit of research, from haunting libraries to midnight sessions with a dozen ancient newspapers, provided no insight to censorship problems with radio shows such as *Little Orphan Annie*, *Burns and Allen*, Arch Obler's splendid *Lights Out* series, or *Inner Sanctum*. But that, in itself, presents us with a lesson. Anyone familiar with the latter two programs will attest to the fact that they are still as strong, if not more so, than the horror of today, whether it be in books or movies. Goose bumps to remember. Why then, was there not a barrage of outraged cries to ban these programs? Simple. Because families listened to these things together.

You know. Together. As a family.

It would be a cop-out for me to say that you can change the station on the radio, or choose not to buy a record. That's the lesson for those judges of the populace, the Censors.

For us, the lesson is a lot more fun, and may startle you.

Become a fan. If a radio station or group of musicians strikes your fancy, tune in to that station, participate in their contests or discussions when you can, send some letters to your local newspaper expressing your admiration, buy the records shamelessly, profess your approval of the music — c'mon! It's not that hard. Get vocal without becoming a fanatic, anyone can do it! Right now, everyone is still entitled to his or her opinion. Before long though, we may be able to have an opinion only when we're entitled to one. Think about it.

Before the bell rings, I'd like to let you know that letters are most welcome, good or bad. Keep in mind that if you hate what I have to say, I may very well pick apart your written missive without mercy. (Isn't freedom great?)

To the younger members of SPWAO, I leave you with this: Music is entertainment, nothing more. It will not cause you to steal or murder. If your parents, clergymen, or peers feel differently, don't despair. Being underage is something you'll outgrow.

Next time up: We'll have some fun with the Government and answer the burning question: "Is it okay to dynamite Mount Rushmore?"

INTRODUCTION: *Column Four, September/October 1989*

At this point, I considered myself established in the pages of the SPWAO newsletter, and so, to make a long story real short, I went fucking crazy with this column, stomping the guts out of the Federal Government, Donald Wildmon, and anything else unholy.

I began to scream at the readers for being apathetic, demanding their participation in the fight against censorship. I used words that were sarcastic and even hateful, saying *exactly* what I wanted to say. The first essay was quoted, as well as my opinions on abortion, gun-control and flag-burning. These latter three items gave the readers more insight on my personal life than anything I had written before in the column.

In addition, I mentioned a Samuel Butler novel, *Erewhon*, the only thing I had ever read by this author. I did this because I knew John Rosenman loved the works of Butler. If you want to call it kissing-ass, that's good, because that's exactly what I was doing.

If you haven't already, you should read *Erewhon*.

It's a damn good novel.

COLUMN FOUR
September/October 1989

I'll bet most of you didn't realize that we have a new President. No, newer than George Bush.

His name is Donald Wildmon and he's done more for the American Public in one year than George will probably do in the next three. Let me rephrase that — he's done more *to* the American Public. Mr. Wildmon has single-handedly been able to shape, to some degree, what we watch on cable and commercial television, what we see in theatres, what we read in books, and what opinions we express. He's also a publisher, how about that? His magazine, *The AFA Journal*, has a circulation of about 380,000 and does such neat things like report, with enough lurid detail as to make George Romero queasy, every off-color item that's fit to ban. Hell, their section on movie reviews beats even the best reviews in *Hustler*. You know, half-limp, fully erect, and so on. Wildmon is actually the best promoter of the things he would like to wipe out, because, you see, most of his readers would never dream of seeing or reading the products of which he presents graphic accounts in *The AFA Journal*.

In an essay I wrote entitled "The Last Temptation and The Day After," I cited Wildmon as the leader of the current censorship threat, as he was at the forefront of the controversy surrounding *The Last Temptation of Christ*, which, by the way, is now available on videocassette. Here's a sampling of the latest prime-time television fare Wildmon would like to see fade to black: *The Wonder Years*, *60 Minutes*, *Highway To Heaven*, *Magical World of Disney*, *Murder, She Wrote*, and *LA Law*. A more complete list appears in the October issue of *Playboy*. Now, I'll bet you didn't know we had a new Vice-President, either. (In fact, you may not be aware we have a Vice-President at all since Bush came into office.)

His name is Jesse Helms, and he's a Senator, which makes him a lot closer to the Vice-President than we'd like to imagine.

And he *loves* artists. Hey, all you artists out there, isn't that nice? Senator Helms so loves art that he, along with a number of other Senators who support him, is trying to push for funding cuts and strict guidelines for the National Endowment for the Arts. What's really funny is that he's going to get what he wants. The NEA has already buckled under and canceled several shows because Helms — *one man* — found the content to be offensive, and therefore objectionable, and therefore not worth anything to anybody. Don't blame the NEA folks, they rely on Government funds to help artists from all walks of life. Blame yourselves, me included. *We're* at fault, we elected that idiot, we checked the little box in the private booth, saying, in essence, "Sure, go ahead, shit on any artist you don't like, we don't care." Oh, but you just draw fantasy images, eh? Maybe a little horror, monsters and stuff, right? Nothing pornographic, or even remotely so, right? Well, it's time to get with the goddamn program. These people aren't playing a game, they're playing with our freedom, they're playing with the ideals that set America apart from any other country in the world. *The Magical World of Disney*, for Christ's sake! And they're serious!

Way back when, I fired a written bullet to this newsletter voicing my opinion on the Ron Leming scandal. Ron had created two images that were discovered to have been based on earlier creations by other artists/photographers in different publications. My letter was in direct opposition to Ron's stance on the subject. I'm sure he's sick of the whole mess, and would like just to forget about the whole thing which, ultimately, was blown way out of proportion.

And I'm sure of a few things about the incident myself. One thing is that I enjoy Ron's art, always have — I think he's one of the best in the Small Press field. His creations are well-crafted, distinctive, sometimes shocking in their interpretations of our world, but all are worthy of a long look. Someday, I would like to meet Ron Leming, or, at the very least, be present at an auction where his original art is offered. Now, my opinion of the situation I mentioned has not changed, nor, I'm sure, has Ron's. But the fact that I was able to disagree with Ron with no thought of damaging his career is quite normal. Do you think that Ron, or any artist who sincerely believes in what he or she is doing, should be able to get a grant to create a masterwork for the public?

So do I.

But, instead, here's what we've got.

We've got a Supreme Court who told the liberals it was okay to burn the American flag in protest, hoping that this would quiet them down when they made the *important* decision to start getting abortion out of the hospitals and back into the alleys. We've got a President who won the election because of his opinions on abortion, not what he could do for the country, which is a good thing, because he's done diddley so far. We've got special interest groups, such as Donald Wildmon, who use terrorist tactics to successfully silence those things they don't care for. Where does that leave us? I don't care for 25% of my paycheck going for nuclear weapons — I'd rather be able to choose where my taxes go. I'd give half to local coalitions for literacy and the other half to the town where I live. Or maybe I'd give it to the National Endowment for the Arts. Many people ask why I'm for abortion, why I'm for flag-burning, why I oppose banning semi-automatic weapons, why I'm such an asshole. My response is the same, whether it be family member, community member, or friend.

I'm not for abortion, I'm for Freedom of Choice. I'm not for flag-burning, would never do it myself, but I don't think someone should spend tangible time in jail for burning a tangible piece of cloth that represents an intangible abstract ideal that is supposed to protect our right to burn the goddamn thing. Freedom is not cheap. I oppose banning semi-automatic weapons because only law-abiding citizens who own these guns will suffer, not drug-dealers who don't give a shit about this law anyway. Last, but not least, I'm an asshole, but that's a matter of opinion. My Mom thinks I'm an okay guy.

President Wildmon and Vice-President Helms are doing a good job of keeping us down. How dare we be creative, anyway? How dare we draw or write or say something that offends them. How dare we? What's wrong with us? Maybe Coventry isn't such a bad idea after all. Yeah, that's it. Isolated camps for anyone who dares to be individual. Samuel Butler wrote about it in *Erewhon*, but since we burned all the copies, we can't read the book.

It's coming, babies, it's at the edge of your town, and you'd better be prepared to settle into some meaningless job and forget you ever had any individual impulses. If you're a musician, stop playing, if you're an artist, stop drawing, if you're a writer, stop writing. That's just a hobby and you won't need a hobby in the New World. It might offend someone with more power than you.

Kinda makes the fact that *Guns 'N Roses* says "fuck" in every other song a little insignificant, doesn't it?

INTRODUCTION: *Column Five, November/December 1989*

This time, I came dangerously close to playing all my cards too early in the game. I attacked two extremes and defended them, citing my reasons throughout the column.

Things began to happen about now.

The SPWAO newsletter this column appeared in also contained several letters in the *Feedback* section concerning Censorship. A couple of the letters shattered my notion that Everybody Loved The Column.

Oh, well.

Life is rough, get a fucking helmet.

COLUMN FIVE
November/December 1989

Extremes in thought this time.

Are some things better left to the censors? Things like child pornography in books and videos, snuff movies (for the naive readers, these are flicks in which someone, usually a woman, is actually killed on camera, usually during sex.), white supremacists on cable, Satanists on cable, communists on cable, ridiculously graphic violence on the page or in the video store — do you see where this list is heading?

Folks, for your information, the two items that probably bristled your neck hairs the most, child pornography and snuff movies are not only readily available to anyone with the inclination to seek them out, they are also very illegal to even own, much less produce. To be quite honest, I've always harbored a secret desire to see a snuff movie, but I don't imagine it would be much different than watching any film by Wes Craven or Tobe Hooper. For me, death isn't much more than an abstract concept at this point in my life. I suppose, however, that if my wife was out of town for a few days and I came across a snuff movie with her in it, I would feel differently.

On the surface, it would appear that my glib comments echo the sentiment of the Cole Porter song, *Anything Goes*.

Quite the contrary.

As I've said, child porn and snuff flicks are illegal and, as such, any outcries from any censors on these subjects are superfluous hot air from people who need a cause, any cause, to bitch about. Last time I checked, the FBI was doing a good job of closing both enterprises down.

So, whaddaya think? Are some things better left to the censors?

Many people use profanity in their daily life, in their art, in their anger, etc. But for every one of us, there is a dozen of them. This is a touchy subject on both sides, kind of like the smoking issue. Well, I'm really deeply, *sincerely* sorry, but I do both. Yep. Both of them. Not only do I wallow in profanity, but I smoke about 40 cigarettes per day. However, I respect those in restaurants, refraining from smoking entirely in a public eating place. In other cases, I respect the No Smoking areas and feed my habit in those nasty "Designated Areas". My penchant for profanity, however, sometimes just creeps out, much to my chagrin. If someone professes an outright dislike for it, I try my best to contain it, again, out of respect. Then again, I don't like to be told twice — I'm smart enough to catch it the first time. Sometimes I even head it off at the pass. Like when I'm eating Thanksgiving dinner with my in-laws.

The parallel between smoking and profanity is clear-cut, it seems, with the bottom line being respect. But, and this is a big but, if someone feels that respect is not enough, that they have to crush any ideal of freedom which they feel differs from their own, then the whole system goes to hell. And that, my friends, is exactly what's at the heart of censorship. In fact, that's why this nightmarish vision is fast becoming a reality. Censors have no respect for you — they have a narcissistic view of themselves, much like Hitler, much like McCarthy, much like Khomeini — little maggots who find themselves with enough power to become big flies and land on anything they think is shit and eat it up. The contemporaries of the three listed above are, without question, Donald Wildmon, Jesse Helms, and Tipper "I Love Rock and Roll" Gore. Their victims are anyone who buckles under, merchant or otherwise, to their terrorist tactics which include threats, boycotts, and old-time "Lynch the niggers" town meetings. Their stormtroopers are in every small town and big city in America. They're doing something about their position. What the hell are you doing about yours? And if you don't believe that these people pull this kind of bullshit, incur their wrath and find out.

So, let's answer that question, at long last.

Are some things better left to the censors?

No.

I promised a few columns ago to list some books, movies, addresses, etc., that might interest you, but then I decided to be mean and just feed you small doses from my censorship stockpile. Call it job security. Hell, call it anything you want. After all, babies, that's still your right.

The Last Temptation of Christ is now out on home video and is currently being run on Cinemax. Write this fellow and applaud him for not buckling under. He caught a lot of heat for his decisions regarding this and would appreciate a kind note.

Tom Pollock, Chairman
MCA, INC
100 Universal City Plaza
Universal City, CA 91608

Now, if you're not moved to write this next fellow, offer your support, and subscribe to his magazine, you shouldn't call yourself an artist, writer, or fan, because you're none of the above.

Gauntlet
Exploring the Limits of Free Expression
Barry Hoffman, Publisher
309 Powell Road
Springfield, PA 19064

We're going to war people. Stay free.

INTRODUCTION:
Column Six, January/February 1990

Along with the feeling that my writing was pissing a few members off, I began to get the strange feeling that some crops of hatred were being grown just for me in their mental gardens. I wasn't too concerned at this, however — I figured they were vegetable gardens, anyway. From the letters printed, I selected the two which opposed my opinion and the very existence of the column the most. The other letters were, overall, supportive.

Since I had warned the readers in an earlier column that I might very well quote them and show them no mercy in response to a letter, I thought to myself, "How on Earth can I let them down?" and proceeded to wax philosophical in my rebuttals with all the charm of Lenny Bruce. To this day, I don't feel that I would get into a fistfight with anyone involved in this written exchange should we meet face-to-face. (Providing they wouldn't swing first.) I ended my responses with a "Thanks for writing" farewell, and I would employ this closing up until the last column.

Early on, I decided not to print the letters in this compilation, feeling that my responses give the first-time reader sufficient explanation of the parts of letters I addressed.

COLUMN SIX
January/February 1990

Happy New Year, fellow artists!

Enough of the pleasantries. Listen to this: In 1989, 1,500,000 letters were sent out requesting a boycott of Mennen and Clorox products by the Rev. Donald Wildmon.

In 1989, Sen. Jesse Helms proposed cutting all funding for the National Endowment for the Arts.

In 1989, Rev. Donald Wildmon accused 75% of the current television fare of promoting the following immoral activities: Homosexuality, Bestiality, Voodoo, Suicide, Teen Sex, Illicit Sex, Sexual Bondage, Sex, Incest, Bitchiness, Abortion, Drug Use, Unacceptable Family Arrangements, Unfavorable Christian Portrayal — etc.

In 1989, 200 Christian ministers faced sexual child-abuse charges which are still pending, none of which were reported in Wildmon's *AFA Journal*.

In 1989, no less than three art exhibits were canceled by the NEA due to pressure from Jesse Helms.

Now, I don't have to tie all these little incidents together, except to say that they happened. Perhaps you noticed one that was not reported in the funny papers — that's right — the 200 cases of child abuse by ministers. I have no interest in poking fun at this fact, only to show that what is perceived as good is not necessarily so all the time. Why then, the blatant absence of coverage for these Men of the Cloth? Could it be because so many of them set themselves up as a little bit better than you and me and, being so divine, are immune to the laws and morals of us little people? *Hm.* Could be. I'm not sure.

We are inundated with information, most of it in the form of bad news, every time we turn around. War in Panama, brutal crimes and murders from the "War on Drugs", assassinations of political figures, letter bombs, inflation, deflation, recession and depression. Where does it end and what cause should we support? In the midst of the overkill, it is easy to forget that we are artists and writers in danger of going underground to ply our trade. After all, the person who lives for nothing but a job and a paycheck works a helluva lot less than those of us who work a job in addition to writing a short story or a novel while maintaining a semi-sane home. The difference is that most of us are too tired at the end of the day to write a letter of protest, unlike the guy that simply works a job, comes home, reads *USA Today*, and scribbles a letter in response to something he's read that he doesn't agree with. That's easy. But we suffer for it. Hey, nobody told us our creative pursuits would be easy, did they?

There has been some talk about SPWAO issuing an "official statement" on censorship. After much thought, I must cast my vote against this idea, as censorship is an individual matter, based on individual choice — if you like it, fine. Watch it, read it, buy it, tune it in. If you don't — don't.

Which brings us to the fun part of this column.

Letter, we get letters.

Rick Lawler wrote a very intelligent letter that provoked much thought as I read, then reread, his words. However, his major point of contention seems to be his objection to his tax dollars supporting something, by his definition, that is less than art. He says, quote, "*...if the Government pays you money, you do what the Government wants...*" I guess I should have included a complete run-down of how exactly the NEA operates. First, the NEA awards grants to artists to create works that will appeal to public sensibilities. Second, the NEA can (and often does) say "Nope, sorry, try something else, this won't cut it." Mr. Lawler also states, in part, that "*...if I want to be a doctor, should I expect the Government to support me just so I can practice my trade badly*?" Well, sad but true, this does happen. Certain (but by no means all) doctors do practice their trade badly for the Government. They're called Civil Servants. In fact, Mr, Lawler, the Government also hires nurses, secretaries, purchasing agents, accountants, writers, managers, etc. But the NEA *does not* hire artists. They award loans or grants, much like college loans. And, as I said before, these can and have been rescinded at times. But, like in any job, you have Government employees with a strange little bugaboo called *Bad Judgment*. I think it's sad to the point of being pathetic that the track record of the NEA, rich with success and supportive of major art galleries across the country that bring pleasure to young and old, liberal and conservative alike, is forgotten because one person handed them a jar filled with a crucifix and piss.

Thanks for writing, Mr. Lawler. You made several other fine points too numerous to mention here, even though I brought up only those I disagree with.

Ron Blizzard was also kind enough to drop a line, stating that I've "paradoxically" attacked people's right to protest against movies, citing *The Last Temptation of Christ* in his indictment. Mr. Blizzard, I defy you to find a single passage in any of my columns where I commit this heinous crime. I have attacked calls for bans and boycotts on both sides of the issue, period. You also asked me if I would think it "art" if someone dropped a Star of David in a bottle of urine. Sorry to disappoint you but, personally, I don't think anything submerged in piss is art. I'm curious though, as to why you picked the Star of David. Do you think I'm Jewish? You're right. I'm a Jewish female who also happens to be black. I also raise pit bulls. Boy, I'll bet your blood's boiling now, huh? By the way, you're wrong about the Federal Government prosecuting you had you dropped said Star in said Jar. Also, you admit you don't know who Donald Wildmon is. Is that true, or were you just making a joke? I hope it was the latter, especially since you're an Editor. You say you like the Small Press because there is freedom of thought, yet you don't consider it a forum for soapbox preaching about the right to insult people. What, exactly, is your definition of "freedom of thought" and where do you find cases of rampant libel, or libel at all, in this column or the newsletter as a whole? Mr. Blizzard, if you don't like the column, then either comprehend what I write so the next time you can send an intelligent letter, or don't read the fucking thing. Thanks for writing.

Oh, I almost forgot.

In 1989, an art exhibit by Robert Mapplethorpe was canceled due to pressure from Helms and his followers. Apparently, Helms didn't like seeing a dick on a male nude, therefore, he deemed it obscene.

In 1989, several towns in Kansas effectively pressured their local cable companies to drop *The Last Temptation of Christ* portion of Cinemax, thereby filling all homes subscribing to the service with two hours of dead time throughout the month of October.

And how was *your* year?

INTRODUCTION:
Column Seven, March/April 1990

This column was written shortly after I had closed the deal on a screenplay sale and had observed the wheels of the Motion Picture Machine start to grind, painfully slow at first, gradually working into a spinning frenzy, sending sparks flying and nerves shattering.

In Kansas City, a scant 20 miles from my home, people were protesting second-runs of *The Last Temptation of Christ* and in Washington, DC, 2000 miles from my home, politicians were deciding whether or not to follow the guidelines of Communism and jail anyone who would insult or deface a symbol of America, land of the free (and also freedom of speech and expression in case you've forgotten).

So, after a brief conversation with Mike Mickes, whom you will meet shortly, I decided to use this personal experience as the vehicle for the next installment.

I'm sorry that I can't report a happy ending to the tale; namely, because it hasn't ended as of this writing. I'm also *real* sorry that I don't have unlimited space to fill you in on some other great anecdotes about Life in the Slow Lane of screenwriting.

Ah, well.

That's entertainment.

COLUMN SEVEN
March/April 1990

From the Moviegoer's standpoint, a motion picture gains approval when it contains interesting characters, clarity of content, and a brisk pace. A feeling that follows the Moviegoer home long after they have tossed the empty cardboard barrel of popcorn into the proper receptacle at the theatre isn't bad either. Unless concerned about their children, or other young people entrusted to their care who will view the picture, the average adult Moviegoer is not too concerned about a four-second shot of human nudity; less so about some profane dialogue. And if they are, they will do one thing, and one thing only — they will not go see the movie. Keep in mind that I have just profiled the Intelligent Moviegoer.

Now, let's talk about the Moron Moviegoer, a person who doesn't need to see a movie before they pass on their opinion to all of us doomed fools. In fact, they will refuse adamantly to view the movie in question, citing one, or a combination of the following three reasons:

1) Too much violence
2) Too much sex
3) Too sacrilegious

In order, the Intelligent Moviegoer realizes that there is more violence in the current push by George Bush to fuck up our Constitution than in any slasher movie.

On the other hand, the Moron Moviegoer thinks that we should do away with *Friday the 13th* (all parts), and jail anyone who dares to put a Bic to the piece of cloth that stands for freedom.

The Intelligent Moviegoer realizes that sex is necessary to further the plot in some movies, but can be used to excess, at which point, it inhibits the scope of the picture. The Moron Moviegoer thinks that sex in movies is wrong, period. For these people, art imitates life.

Religion is a part of life, but a very personal part, based on individual interpretation of faith. The Intelligent Moviegoer knows this. The Moron Moviegoer, however, knows that movies such as *The Last Temptation of Christ* serve only one purpose; namely to piss them off. Even though most protesters have never seen the movie, they can't let Jesus and his Heavenly Father be offended, so they set themselves up as a buffer between God and us poor, misguided, Intelligent Moviegoers. They gather together and boycott, ban, and threaten, all in the name of religion. You know. Like what Hitler did — "We're the Master Race and we've got ovens for everyone else."

The Intelligent Moviegoer sees a movie he or she doesn't like, so he or she doesn't recommend it. The Moron Moviegoer not only doesn't like the movie, he or she wants to burn down the theatre and have the actors and actresses blacklisted. Sound familiar? I hope it does. But just in case it doesn't, allow me to remind you of Smokin' Joe McCarthy, whose Communist hunt rampaged through Hollywood in the 50's, slaying all in its path, which was damn near every working human being in Tinsel Town at that time. The result: Less creative efforts and, statistically more ruined lives and livelihoods than any Baby Boomer can imagine. People lost their jobs, were forced to move themselves and their families with nowhere to go, were refused work, regardless of the work's merit, stopped writing, stopped trying to write, stopped hoping for work period. That was almost forty years ago, so who gives a shit, huh? Couldn't happen now, right?

I hope to Goodness that the readers of this column are not so incredibly naive as to actually subscribe to this way of thinking, this apathetic, blind attitude that serves only to inject rust into an already festering sore in Freedom's body. I'm not a self appointed God of moral freedom and this newsletter didn't recruit me as such. I'm just one little guy speaking out against something going on that's very, very wrong. It's okay to disagree with the words, it's okay to point out the mistakes. But you'd better get the message, because the message is right: Censorship is wrong in America. This is where we live, after all. And, like the founders of the country, we've got to start somewhere.

Now that you're all warmed up and all set to go to the movies, hop in. I'll drive.

I had the privilege of watching the Motion Picture Association of America (MPAA) work a few weeks ago, doing what they do best: assign a letter rating to a movie. Although the movie in question contained no nudity, little profanity, and no violence, and is aimed largely at the eighteen and under crowd, the MPAA defended their preliminary decision of slapping the movie with an "R" rating based on the following: The movie, it seems, graphically depicts cocaine use, and is, in fact, the focal point of the entire movie.

Michael Mickes, President of Upward Bound productions, had this to say in rebuttal: "The movie does show drug use — in an extremely unfavorable light. This, coupled with the setting — a rock band on their way to stardom — is, in my opinion, a very good vehicle for young teens. It doesn't preach, it doesn't threaten jail time, it shows, in a very realistic light, what can happen to a life when a drug becomes the only goal."

Although just passing pre-production with a couple of rushes in the can and a dozen binders full of permits, ledgers, and contracts, Mickes explained that if stuck with an "R" rating, he will have to do one of three things: Release the movie without a rating, in which case no newspaper will carry an ad for it, slash scenes until the MPAA decides to grant a PG-13, in which case the entire message of the movie will come across as diluted and therefore ineffective, or accept the "R" rating, in which case the very audience the movie is intended for will have to sneak into theatres like Miniature Mall Criminals, or worse yet, will not get to see the movie at all. Because, contrary to what Wildmon, Helms, Gore, and a hornet's nest of others would have you believe, there are actually good parents out there. I remember sitting with my Grandparents and watching *All in the Family* while my parents attended a late showing of *The Exorcist*, much to my dismay. Jesus, out of the frying pan and into the fire, huh?

I really hope that Mickes is able to sway the MPAA when the final product is reviewed. I have my doubts however. You see, his screenwriter has a horrible reputation of saying the right thing at the wrong time. Yeah, you guessed it. Me. Someday, maybe a few synapses in my brain will burn out and I'll be able to do nice, innocuous work, like staff writer for Walt Disney. Nah, that wouldn't work. Wildmon hates them, too.

Next up: Say goodbye to the NEA.

Until then, I'll see you at the movies. I hope.

INTRODUCTION:
Column Eight, May/June 1990

My personal philosophy on the censorship issue had now emerged from its chrysalis and spread its newfound wings. I began to act on the things I read about, attempting to secure individual statements right up to full-blown interviews with no experience whatsoever in acquiring or conducting these verbal exchanges. Accordingly, I took issue with the viewpoints of other creative artists, berating them for their short-sightedness on an issue that had become larger-than-life, both inside and outside the pages of the SPWAO newsletter.

Around this time, I spent innumerable hours searching for and finally discovering the book-form of Robert Mapplethorpe's art, quite surprised to see included in his "vulgar" works, portraits of Richard Gere, Arnold Schwarzennegger, and other still-life photography.

If you didn't catch the joke in that last line, shame on you. You must be asleep.

This column generated a lively, if largely one-dimensional debate with the battle-cry being "I Don't Like My Tax Dollars Going For Art I Don't Like," which, I guess, is cool. After all, these same people, along with me, probably don't like their tax dollars going to fund bounced checks by scumbag Senators and Congressmen who should be spending time in Federal Prison along with their constituents who are guilty of nothing more or less, except that they were held accountable. In addition, these same people, unlike me, probably have never voiced their concern over the rampant corruption of their elected officials.

Likewise, the issue over "sexist" jokes. I am utterly amazed at the likes of comedian Jay Leno who thinks that these jokes, along with ethnic jokes, are "thoroughly disgusting and have no place in comedy". Don't worry, Jay, they'll also make more comedians. I'm not the sharpest person on the face of the Earth, not by a longshot, but even I realize that the operative word in a sexist joke or an ethnic joke, or any other joke for that matter, is "*joke.*" A joke pokes fun at a stereotype, holding it up in the light of humor for the purpose of revealing how wrong, to the point of being funny, the stereotype actually is.

Now, personally, I don't like jokes that start with "Steve Beai is such an asshole that...." or "Steve Beai was sucking dick one day when...." Do you get the picture? If a joke is told about a housewife, a two-dollar whore, a pollock, a nigger, an Italian, or a farmer's daughter, for God's sake, they're not talking about *you*.

Even though today it's fashionable, even chic to call yourself a victim, the glaring truth of the matter is that there are very few actual victims in this arena of discrimination.

Lighten up, people.

COLUMN EIGHT
May/June 1990

This time, I had hoped to interview John Frohnmayer, Chairman for the National Endowment for the Arts, in order to get a little better perspective on the NEA's stand supporting the Mapplethorpe exhibit now careening its way across the country, striking fear into the hearts of millions.

No such luck.

I phoned the Executive offices of the NEA in Washington, DC and was informed by a receptionist that I would have to make an appointment. Quite a trick since I was 2000 miles away. I explained this simple fact of geography and was told, once again, that I would have to make an appointment. *How do I go about making an appointment?* I inquired. I was told that I would have to speak to Mr. Frohnmayer to set one up. *That's what I'm trying to do* I told the receptionist. The receptionist informed me that Mr. Frohnmayer was in a meeting and that I would have to call back later. Radical, eh, Dude? So, after burning up many favors and preparing a nifty little package outlining my credentials and intent, I faxed the entire thing to Mr. Frohnmayer's fax machine, receiving a curt and courteous reply that Mr. Frohnmayer had said everything he had to say on the Mapplethorpe controversy, thank you anyway.

Now, then.

Those of you who hate this column, but read it anyway, are probably laughing. Those of you who love this column and force yourselves to read it are probably laughing, too. After all, that situation *is* funny: I attempted to reach a person in a position of power for a Government-sanctioned program who has come under fire from the very forces that put him in that position. So, what happens? He balks, thinking it's best to keep quiet. Granted, he was vocal in the *USA Today* interview, but what did he really say? For those of you who read the 200-word interview — answer the question. For those of you who didn't — keep quiet and read on, because this column is for you. Here it goes.

Frohnmayer said nothing, basically, admitting that he hadn't even seen the exhibit in question. *But* — he felt that the issue should be left up to individuals to decide. Now I agree with those last few words as I'm sure you all do. It's what he didn't say that made him seem a little uninformed, or, worse yet, unconcerned. *Example:* SPWAO members, are you for creative freedom? *Answer:* Of course you are. *Example:* Do you think that Sinead O' Conner and Nora Dunn were correct in their opposition and boycott of Andrew "Dice" Clay's appearance on Saturday Night Live? Or are they just adding fuel to the censorship bonfire? *Answer:* You tell me.

I happen to think that Clay is arrogant and chauvinistic, much like Sam Kinison, but I also think that Nora Dunn is a creative hypocrite — she can poke fun at public figures such as Bush, Noriega, Taylor, et.al., but if someone pokes fun at her — look out. Sinead O' Connor summed up the reason for her personal boycott as this: "It would be nonsensical to sing about a woman's experiences after a monologue by Clay." Why is that? Clay, abrasive as he is, talks about a male bigot's experience with women, much like Archie Bunker did. My personal opinion of Nora Dunn is that she is funny, along with my opinion of Clay; he's funny, too. My opinion about Sinead O' Connor is that she sings about women's experiences because she's probably had a lot of them, being somewhat of a woman herself. Don't like that, huh? Then stop here and read another column in the newsletter.

If you're still with me, remember this about bans and boycotts: Agree, don't idolize. Disagree, don't hate. In the final analysis, people, it takes all kinds to make up a world. And while everyone should and does have a right to disagree, a right to an opinion for or against a certain thing, it is quite another matter for one to think he or she has the right to wipe whatever he or she doesn't like off the face of the Earth. Of course, this philosophy doesn't apply to noxious weeds such as Thistles, Poison Ivy, or those big spiders that build a huge web between the house and the tree and wait at night for you to run your face right into them.

The Diceman characterizes women as "walking brooms", "whores", etc. While I may not subscribe to that way of thinking, I'll be damned if some asshole with a Government job or Politician for a husband is going to decide that I don't need to see such things. Oh, I forgot to mention another group — creative artists who are jumping on the bandwagon of boycotts.

Andrew Clay doesn't *live* with me. He's just a guest. When I'm tired of his company, I just turn the television off. It's amazing that there are still people around who haven't quite mastered that most simplest of exercises that technology hath wrought; it takes one finger, or one foot, or maybe a baseball bat, but we are all capable of turning off the offending appliance, be it a television, radio, or cheap toaster. Hey, nobody forced us to buy these things in the first place.

The heart of the Saturday Night Live controversy and, to a lesser degree, the Mapplethorpe issue, seems to be centered around racism. On one hand, you have people who want to wipe out the Mapplethorpe exhibit because they don't like homosexuals. (And don't try to use that stupid argument about Mapplethorpe's "kiddie-porn" photos — the two photos in question are very tasteful. Unless you're against any unclothed human form.) Is Clay a racist? If you think so, don't watch him, don't listen to him, don't speak his name, don't take up sculpture as a hobby unless you use marble. Are Mapplethorpe's photos disgusting? Fine, don't go to the exhibit, and, whatever you do, don't buy the book of the exhibit. (29.95, in the Arts section at any bookstore — Waldenbooks reports brisk sales — my personal opinion: Disappointed. It was made out to be more disgusting than it really is. A real letdown for me.) It's really quite a funny paradox that the people who want to eradicate all things immoral, obscene, racist, and disgusting are the very people who are thrusting these things into the public light, giving them greater exposure than imagined. How many 60-70 year-old men and women do you think know who Andrew "Dice" Clay is? How many do you think really care? How many people in general know how many horrible things are warping our minds whenever we watch *Alf* or *The Simpsons*? Thanks to the likes of Donald Wildmon, we all know. How nice to be informed. Hey, maybe we should all become just like the censors.

Now *that's* a paradox for you. A terrifying one.

INTRODUCTION: Column Nine, July/August 1990

At this point, I had received so many crank letters from nutcases, that I began to look forward to what the mailman would bring next in the form of missives from the maladjusted among us.

Censorship had taken root as an important issue with the SPWAO members — I just figured everyone was tuning into the same broadcasts I had been monitoring for almost a year. Never, for even a second, did I consider that my column was the source of this newfound awareness from these people.

One of the letters I came across in my mailbox, actually a package, was from Bob Crouch in Pittsburg, Kansas. Now, there are very few people I have come across in that big state whom I consider to be enlightened artistically, much less intelligent. Since Bob Crouch's envelope was written with a *pencil*, I figured that his correspondence would be no different than the myriad of other FANatic mail I had the pleasure to read.

I was dead wrong.

Bob had sent me a copy of his outstanding small press magazine *The Obligatory Sin*, along with a friendly letter suggesting that I might want to submit something for his consideration. Since I had been unable to interview the Chairman of the NEA, as reported in the previous column, I came up with the idea of interviewing Bob. After all, he was an Editor in the Small Press, someone with whom the members could relate. A few written exchanges later, he agreed, and we conducted the interview entirely by mail. I have never met or talked with Bob, but I believe that the measure of a man is in the words that he keeps. And Bob Crouch certainly measures right up there with the best of them.

After you read what follows, I'm sure you'll agree.

COLUMN NINE
July/August 1990

Welcome to the Dog Days of summer. Since your blood's already boiling from the seasonal heat, I thought it might be nice to give you a chance to cool off in my own special way. So pour yourself another glass of lemonade, crack open that beer, mix them both together and drink it down. Here we go.

Instead of listening to my usual malevolent tirades, this time you get to hear from someone else.

Bob Crouch, Editor of *The Obligatory Sin*, graciously consented to share his thoughts with us concerning censorship among the Small Press and beyond. Mr. Crouch has managed to attract such notables to the pages of TOS as Ree Young, Marge Simon, Cathy Buburuz, and *Heavy Metal* artist Bucky Montgomery, to name just a few. An excellent artist in his own right, Bob is currently waging a most unique war on the stifling of creative freedom.

SB: How was *The Obligatory Sin* conceived?

Bob Crouch: I originally wanted TOS to be a Fantasy and Surrealistic art magazine to help those who needed an outlet for publishing their work. I received a lot more literature than art, so the current format was born! The title refers to my all-consuming need to create. Art is my mistress and little else outshines her.

SB: Did you ever anticipate, or hope for, any negative reactions regarding content?

BC: There have been people who have had a negative reaction to the title without ever reading the magazine, and I anticipated that. I did not start TOS with the idea of shocking people. I wanted the magazine to represent the artist's and writer's own ideas regarding the themes I select, whether I agree with them or not. Negative reactions may be a by-product of reading TOS, but I don't select stories on that basis.

SB: Have you had any personal experience with censorship relating to *The Obligatory Sin*?

BC: Besides people accusing TOS of having a Satanic title, I've only had one incident that I would consider a form of censorship. A person I work with purchased issue #3, False Prophets. He and his roommate read it and then had a little book-burning ceremony, denouncing TOS as a work of the Devil. I found this to be both sad and humorous.

SB: One might argue that since the issue was sold, the owner of the issue could do with it as they saw fit.

BC: They sure can! However, they really missed the boat completely. Issue #3 exposes False Prophets — it does not celebrate them. Some of TOS contributors have been clergy members. I find it ironic so many people see Satanic worship within the stories and poems.

SB: Currently, there's a big push against so-called "Satanism", an idea as old as the idea of Christianity. Do you think this trend has given re-birth to the "witch-hunters" of old, willing to condemn and destroy anything they perceive as even remotely in conflict with their individual beliefs?

BC: I'm not sure that this "trend" has ever disappeared. What I fear about these "protectors of morality" is that, well, who is going to protect me from them?

SB: You've started a unique campaign against censorship that a few Small Press publications have supported. Could you elaborate on this?

BC: It would be wrong of me to state that I am against all acts of censorship. Child porn, I think, is very bad. I am, however, against the ones that go against my enjoyments in life. One of my enjoyments is Heavy Metal music. This form of music has been very much attacked in the last few years, being labeled as "Satanic". True, Heavy Metal has Satanic overtones, but keep in mind that this is just an act, a fantasy played out on a stage. Too many people confuse fantasy with reality. My idea of "Give a Bang for Liberty" defends not only my love for Metal music but the Visual Arts, as well. I got the idea from Metal music also being called "Head-Banging" music. With the Liberty Bell being a symbol of freedom, I thought — "Bang your head on the Liberty Bell and let freedom ring". That doesn't mean that I want someone to go out and actually do that, it just means defend your rights or someone will take them away. Remember that, although *1984* has come to pass, the possibility of a Big Brother has not.

SB: With the appearance of Barry Hoffman's *Gauntlet*, the outcry from citizens in Cincinnati against the attempted censorship of the Mapplethorpe art exhibit, your own efforts, etc., it is obvious that people are becoming more concerned with the issue of artistic censorship. What can the individual artist/writer do to make his voice heard?

BC: Attend city council meetings whenever they concern issues related to censorship. Publish work that supports your ideas. Don't be afraid to make a statement, there are many outlets for you. Put your work in anti-censorship publications.

SB: What defense do Editors have against pressure from a group wanting to censor their publication?

BC: Small Press is unique in that many of our readers share our ideas and are very open-minded. Our magazines are published out of love for art and literature, not just for money. Your best defense is to publish what you want, what you feel is best, and speak out publicly against values you don't agree with. It is astounding to me that the pro-censorship people don't submit stories, poems, and art for publication in magazines that they consider unfit. I would be interested in seeing their work. Plus, they would be making a more powerful impact, in a more positive manner.

SB: Any advice for the apathetic among us who feel the problem is not that bad?

BC: The whole problem with censorship is that what offends one person does not offend his neighbor. If you are not offended by the censorship problem, you have two choices: One — go ahead and ignore it, but don't bitch if all your freedoms are taken away! Two — Defend your rights! Maybe the porn shop is being closed down the block and you feel that's OK. But don't wait until R rated movies are pulled out of theatres. Be vigilant at all times, be ready to act on your conscience.

SB: Yes, it's me again. I'd like to thank Bob Crouch for taking the time to share his insights with us. Now for the big finish — until I see you in the fall, stay cool.

Subscriptions and queries to *The Obligatory Sin* should be addressed to Bob Crouch, 210 E. Jefferson, Pittsburg, KS 66762. Unfortunately, issue #3, False Prophets, is sold out. Issues #4 & #5 will be combined into a big double issue (approx. 90-100 pages). A section on censorship will be included and is currently open for poems, art, and short comments. Advance orders, $4.00 each, after publication, $5.00 each. Rights revert to contributors after publication.

Gauntlet reports an "underwhelming" response from SPWAO members, although issue #1 (containing work from Harlan Ellison, Gary Brandner, et al) is selling briskly. C'mon, guys, check out what everyone else already knows! Issue #2 will probably adopt a trade paperback format to accommodate the flood of commentary from writers you see on Bestseller lists. Don't be left in the dust! Write: Gauntlet, INC, Dept. GA2, 309 Powell Road, Springfield, PA 19064.

Disclaimer: The latter commercial announcements are *not* endorsed by the American Family Association, Parent's Music Resource Center, the Chief of Police in Cincinnati, Jesse Helms, any Kleagle of the Ku Klux Klan, any member of the Skinheads, Crips, or Bloods, George Bush, Kurt Waldheim, or Adolph Hitler.

And we're glad.

INTRODUCTION:
Column Ten, September/October 1990

There are very few people with whom I've ridden the edge with, and none with the spirit of Mike Olson. I first met Mike through SPWAO's First Contact Committee, a group of volunteers who write welcome letters and provide information to all new members. Mike was heading up the project, and I had volunteered my time to him. We quickly started a correspondence that developed into a deep friendship that has endured to this day. Mike was eventually elected President of SPWAO and he solicited me for the job of Treasurer, which I readily accepted.

Shortly after I began Censoring the Censors, Mike had his own column — Copyright Basics — in which he presented a wealth of information gleaned from copyright law and Government rulings on the issue, as well as personal anecdotes, well-known cases that established precedents in this area, etc. One afternoon, late in the summer of 1990, Mike called me and we shot the shit for awhile, discussing everything from the movies we had recently seen, to books we recommended to each other to read. I had been putting the final touches on a novel and was grateful for the break. I sat and listened and talked, gazing absently out of my office window. Suddenly, the tone of Mike's voice dropped an octave, as it always does when Mike is contemplating mischief. My attention focused on his words and I wondered what strange and terrible thing we were about to get involved in now.

"We ought to write each other's columns next month and see if anyone notices," he said simply.

I laughed. "But we should try to imitate the other's style if we don't want anyone to notice."

"Absolutely," he said.

So, Mike contacted John Rosenman, who quickly agreed, not wanting to be left out of the fun, and the following column was born. I did not read this column prior to publication in the newsletter, trusting Mike's wealth of talent to pull it off in style. And he certainly did.

It is interesting to note that Mike never received any scathing letters directed at his effort, while I was challenged for my version of Copyright Basics, even though I had reported strictly facts, with no editorializing whatsoever. Hmm. It seems the members noticed after all.

COLUMN TEN
September/October 1990

Did you know that 70% of Egyptian women are unable to achieve orgasm because they have their clitoris removed before they reach puberty? The mothers often seek out the same person who did it to them to sneak up behind their daughters and pin their arms back when they least expect it, often dragging them kicking and screaming to where the little operation is to be performed. I'm told it's a very frightening and painful experience.

Aren't you glad you don't live in Egypt? I bring this up not as an example of Censorship but as an extreme example of the same reason why the actual word *Censorship* sends little waves of disgust to my brain every time I hear it: people telling people what they can and can't do. And as long as there are people living and breathing on this planet, you can bet that there will be other Bible-thumping, self-appointed saviors of the planet, aggressively trying to set limits on just how much walking and talking you should do. Worse for children, of course.

How can you battle censorship in a world where you are accustomed to being censored from the time of your birth on? And yet it is far better that the parents take the responsibility for the child's upbringing than have the government do it for you. In 1984, the Reagan administration deregulated the commercial content of children's programming, only to see new legislation approved recently by the House which would limit the amount of advertising on children's TV shows and require regulators to weigh, in renewing the license of TV stations, how well broadcasters are serving the educational needs of children. What's wrong with that, you ask; after all, as one lawmaker stated, children's TV shows are little better than Toys-R-Us Catalogs these days. But they wouldn't be if the parents who felt that this type of programming was garbage didn't let their kids watch it to begin with, and as far as I'm concerned any censorship is too much. All it does is set a precedent for the next item someone decides is not right for us and needs to be phased out.

Inaction. How is this relevant? Inaction means you go with the flow. Don't rock the boat. Live and let live. Most of us do it. But what about those few who don't ? Do you realize that when the majority of people are content to just sit back and watch the world go by, those *few* suddenly *become* the majority? Does this scare you? It should. It scares me.

Look what has happened to cable television. When cable first came out, part of its attraction was "All types of movies, all the time, 24 hours a day." Take a look at your cable guide now. Aside from the occasional R-rated movie popping up as a prime-time feature, the rest are all slotted in the "After Midnight Zone." What happened? A few outraged parents decided they didn't want their children subjected to sex and violence, joined forces, and protested. Keep in mind, this is when lock-out keys, designed specifically to make channels unavailable to children at the parent's discretion, were still being used.

And they did it. Not enough people bothered to stand up for their right to pay to watch whatever they want *whenever* they want to. The few became the moral majority by process of self-election, and brought the cable companies to their knees. A spokesman for one company said, "Hey, if you spend 8 to 10 hours a day doing nothing but addressing the concerns of an organized opposition, how much time does that leave to do other things? For example: *"Our jobs.*" The sad thing about this, by the time some people did try to block this loss of choice, it was too late. The activists had the momentum. And why be a *responsible* parent, taking the time to oversee what your kids are watching when it's easier to dictate policy for an entire nation and censor what they can watch and when. Well, the VCR companies love these squeaky clean, upstanding, moral mommies. They make a fortune off of them. Inaction. If you are not part of the solution, you are part of the problem.

Inaction is also saying, "Yeah, okay, but what am *I* supposed to do about it?" Well , the last time I looked, the first amendment still gives us the right to freedom of conscience, thought, and the expression of thought through speech, press, peaceable assembly, and petition. That amendment wasn't enacted just for the sake of the censors. It was enacted for all of us. Who's dictating policy for you? Well, Steve has been doing a great job of filling us in on that. If I can accomplish one thing with this article, I would hope to instill in you the belief that censorship affects us all in our daily lives. It' s a beast waiting to strike you in your homes and communities. And while you may be content to sit back and let others worry about the censorship problems, the problems keep growing, feeding off inaction like a shit-breathing dragon festering in the bowels of your very own sewer system. But that's okay cause we can just flush the bastard away, right? See, it's been easy! Just depress this shiny lever and all that bad shit goes right down the toilet. Yeah, right. That's what some people thought before they had to go out and buy a VCR in order to watch their favorite movies without losing a night's sleep.

Do you think that your favorite soap operas don't have to pass a Board of Censors? If you do, you are sadly mistaken. Come on, admit it. Just once, with your children safely ensconced away, wouldn't you like to see Erica Caine and Jack Montgomery totally naked and knocking back the foliage surrounding Palmer Cortland's gazebo, while Travis Montgomery masturbated off in the weeds? Maybe this isn't the best time for jokes, but I know *I* would feel better about having gotten that VCR, if I knew that I had that particular episode on tape. But, hey, that's just me! Apply the same censorship formula to your own viewing needs and desires.

I remember reading, I think in Castlerock, Stephen King's account of how he couldn't buy a men's magazine in a certain town because they had been banned by moral crusaders. I thought at the time that that could never happen here. But it did! It happened right here in Shawano, Wisconsin. Using religion as a springboard, a small group of people united and pressured local retailers into removing "all that terrible pornography." It lasted all of about two weeks. People got fed up real fast, here. But it was still a very enlightening experience. Just last year, the USA Network was removed from our cable line-up and it's still gone. Why? Because the cable company took a poll and most of the subscribers who responded, who also happened to be older, retired folks, told the cable company exactly what the cable company wanted to hear, that they'd rather watch old movies on Turner Network television. You can say that my right to watch USA was and still is effectively censored because of a poll which, in my opinion, was slanted to achieve the desired result. They then came along and tried to smooth things over by saying, "Well, we may pick up the USA Network some time again in the future." Yeah, sure. In my lifetime?

Censorship: It's an ugly concept. But it's also human nature. It's very basic to what and who we are as adults because we grow up with it. And that's what really scares me the most. *We grow up with it*. Inner space novels (in this instance, as opposed to outer space) such as Orwell's *1984* or Brunner's *The Shockwave Rider* and *The Jagged Orbit* depict a future society where the government controls everything through manipulation of the media, pressure to stay within certain guidelines as to what is normal behavior and what is not, etc. But to some extent these books are not merely speculative fiction but extensions of what already *exists* on this planet. Yes, even in the good old USA. So if *Censorship* sends little spikes of displeasure to your cerebrum, as it does me, *Inaction* should make you want to vomit.

INTRODUCTION: *Column Eleven, November/December 1990*

I am afraid of spiders.I have been afraid of spiders as far back as I can remember, even though Harlan, my beautiful Mexican Red-Legs Tarantula has been with me since 1981, guarding my office and providing a sort of twisted companionship for me. Harlan has even managed bite me twice, as a reminder that I shouldn't fuck with her when she wants to be left alone. For reasons I have yet to figure out, I am not afraid of Harlan, nor would I be rendered harmless if someone threw a jar of spiders in my face and then tried to kill me. Afraid of spiders I may be, but I have my priorities straight.

Many of those who wrote letters via the Feedback section in the SPWAO newsletter thought they had that jar of spiders aimed at me and were quite surprised to find out all they had were ladybugs when I stomped the guts out of their poor attempts at literacy.

It never failed to amaze me that every single person who wrote to oppose the column, and a few who wrote to support it, were missing the point entirely, focusing mostly on the messenger rather than the message. Though I'm not fond of class distinctions, they do exist, and the Letter-Writers as a majority fell into two classes, one I found pathetic, and one I found terrifying.

The first class I call the "Need-To-See-My-Name-In-Print" group. These people professed to be "writers of import" when, in reality, they were bitter people with questionable talent who needed an outlet for their free-floating hatred and they found it with Censoring the Censors. The Feedback section in the newsletter provided the vehicle to deliver their frustrations. For the entire run of the column, I can recall only *one* argument that made any sense in the context of the subject matter, that of Rick Lawler. (See Column Six) Overall, this class of Letter-Writers was pathetic.

The second class I call the "Agree-With-Everything-You-Say" group. While it was easy to become drunk on the Strange Wine of "*I love your column and you are right in your interpretation of every issue*", I came to see that these people had missed the point of the columns as well, and were, in fact, more dangerous than those who outright hated what I said. Because, you see, the point of all of the columns was about celebrating *informed* individual choice. I never asked for, nor did I expect blind conformity. This class of people stalk movie stars, professional athletes, and politicians. Don't believe me? Read Stephen King's *Misery* or pick up a paper and read about California's "Stalker Law" that reward these goofy motherfuckers with a prison term when they harass public figures in the name of Fandom.

Around the time I penned this column, I opened my mailbox and found among the bills and junk mail, a neatly wrapped little package with no return address. I rolled it over and over in my hands, finally holding it up to my ear and shaking it.

Much to my dismay, I heard a distinct and constant *tick-tick-tick* coming from inside. No, it wasn't a bomb. It was a clock that my mother had bought for me at a garage sale in Indiana and sent to me. But, hell, I didn't know that, so I threw the sonofabitch as far as I could and dialed 911. Talk about embarrassed.The bottom line is the same now as it was then; if I had been restricted to only one word regarding my opinion on censorship it would have to be "think".

Think.

This has endured as my absolute favorite column.

COLUMN ELEVEN
November/December 1990

In Missouri, along with a few other states in the Midwest, we have a cute little creature called a Brown Recluse. Now, as far as spiders go, the Brown Recluse is small and goes relatively unnoticed by most people here, including the majority of stalwart arachnophobes. This is due, in part, to the fact that they are rarely seen, hence the tag *Recluse*. But...in rural areas they can be observed frequently running around tree trunks, basking carefree on the sides of houses, and hanging suspended right in front of your unsuspecting face. Now, as a dedicated arachnophobic fellow myself, I watch for them with an eagle eye at Darkmoor, and I usually see them but, because they're also *fast*, I have a hard time bagging them which leads to a hard time sleeping at night. Why, you might be asking, does a spider cause me so much grief, and what in the world does this have to do with censorship? Please indulge me while I give a neat two-part answer which, hopefully, will satisfy even the most skeptical and/or bored among you.

There are only two spiders in North America that are highly poisonous. One is the Black Widow, fortunately not common in the Midwest. Unfortunately, the second species is. And that's the Brown Recluse. Worse yet, when you invade this spider's territory, which is usually a folded towel or article of clothing, it will bite, injecting an anesthetic before the venom. Thus, you never know you've been bitten until it's too late.

Do you remember the big stink that Elvis caused by swinging a leg and dry-fucking the stage? *Presto*. Suddenly, Elvis could only be seen from the waist up on television and many places refused to host his concerts. Today, that seems kinda funny, sort of innocuous, doesn't it? We know Elvis, hey, he's the King, right? No matter who you are, or what you believe, Elvis is okee-dokee.

So much for the anesthetic. Now for the sickness.

The National Endowment for the Arts is running scared, so much so, that even the artist who wishes to show the world his or her talent with works depicting wildlife or photos of the human condition (and I mean the homeless, the helpless, the lost, etc.) are finding it hard to gain any support from the Government. Hey, maybe they should just apply for the Welfare program — it's alive and well.

Luther Campbell of *2 Live Crew*, even though exonerated in the eyes of Justice, has been brought to his knees where live performance is concerned. Now, he has said he will not use such explicit language when dealing with the realities of 13-year old girls giving blow-jobs and fucking the night away for a vial of crack, of young men slitting the throats of anyone who gets in their way of making a buck in order to survive in a predatory and poverty-ridden situation, or of late-night gang rapes and coat-hangar parties in alleyways — *however* — Luther Campbell will still try to deliver his message of hope to those in that situation, to show them that there's something more in life, only now he will talk in subtler tones, like Mr. Rogers.

Good luck.

If you don't have a copy of the Crew's *As Nasty As They Wanna Be* album, tough shit. Now you can't find it anywhere. Those who would stifle seem to be of the philosophy that "If you ban it, if you boycott it, and if you ignore it, it will go away." Hell, then it's only a matter of time before teenage pregnancy, drug-abuse, and crime come to an end, right? Don't address it and don't express it and it will just dissolve. *Wow*. A regular revelation.

Here's three quotes from three very different people. I guarantee there's something for everyone here.

Colleen Dewhurst, President, Actor's Equity — "Art, in every form, reflects the human condition of the age in which it is created. At times, the reflection is disturbing. If one chooses to deny that these things are happening around them, it is their prerogative to tune the images out, which include taking responsibility for raising their own children in the environment they see fit. It is not a privilege, nor is it a right to deny others access to these creative reflections of the one world we all live in."

Jesus Christ, Son of God, Savior of Man (as told to Matthew) — "Do not judge, lest you be judged. For in the way you judge, you will be judged; and by your standard of measure, it will be measured to you. And why do you look at the speck that is in your brother's eye, but do not notice the log that is in your own eye?"

Terry Rakolta, President, Americans for Responsible Television (regarding the sitcom Married With Children) — "I was appalled at what I saw being presented on the public airwaves. I, as well as thousands of families across America, have latchkey children and they have access to the television. It's no secret that children get more information from TV than they get from their parents or teachers at school. The television shapes a child's view of the outside world."

There you have it, friends. No comment from me. Think.

Letters, we get letters.

I'd like to thank Mike Olson from taking time out as a part-time Copyright Columnist and full-time Child Pornographer to pen my last column. I hoped he liked my rendition of his as well as I liked his rendition of mine.

T.M. Spell, Editor of the *Couch Potato Journal* called Mapplethorpe's photos of children "Child Erotica" and "...about as tasteful as incest." Well, T.M., the court didn't see it as such, neither did the children's parents, so I must hazard a guess that your analysis of this issue was full of shit. In fact, the mother of one of the kids called the photos "charming". I didn't think the photos were particularly charming but, then again, they're not my kids. As for the analogy to incest, I wouldn't know. Thanks for writing. By the way, your absolute pro-censorship extremism in the form of gibbering rage comes across almost as well as my anti-censorship extremism. Almost, but not quite.

Pamela "Panda" Englerth — Panda, thanks for writing. I can't address your concerns and questions regarding Shannon Riley — that's something she must do herself. What I will try to address is your anxiety on being a Christian where SPWAO is concerned. I would hope that you don't feel isolated because of your religious affiliation, but welcomed because you're part of a creative family. And creativity should and does transcend all personal lifestyles and beliefs. SPWAO is a forum, a private one, if you will, to air gripes and share thoughts in any way possible. If you found some of the writing juvenile, well, that's your right. Everyone's a critic. One exception I must take with your letter is this: Ms. Riley does not condemn boycotts against *violence*. Who would? But, by your own association, you include violence with pornography. We all know what violence is, but just what is pornography? A picture of a nude? A picture of human sexual intercourse? A picture of animal sexual intercourse? Bared breasts, man or woman? Bared pubic hair, man or woman? Bugs Bunny without pants? Where, exactly, do you draw the line, and should a line be drawn at all when dealing with nudity? If, as you say, pornography causes aggression, rape, misdirected lust and exploits women (I won't address child porn as it is illegal and covered in an earlier column) why then, the brutal rapes and murders which occurred before there was ever such a thing as pictures of nudes, i.e. Jack The Ripper, and a thousand other less known, but just as notorious sex criminals? I have never called for outlawing bans and boycotts; surely that is our right, no matter what position we choose to take. But, regarding censorship, if you approve of and attend demonstrations to strongarm merchants to remove an item from their shelf then you are part of the problem, not the solution. Many thanks for the tape of *Armada*, I enjoyed it. And welcome to SPWAO. Your willingness to get involved from the outset of your membership is refreshing!

The Brown Recluse crawling up my wall says it's time to go. He may be small, fast, and poisonous, but I'm going to get the little sonofabitch.

INTRODUCTION
Column Twelve, March 1991

The Joan Cissom/Shannon Riley incident sparked much controversy in the pages of the SPWAO news letter. Briefly, Joan and Shannon were relatives who shared a common interest; that of publishing Small Press horror magazines. Unfortunately, they resided in Wildmon country — short miles away from the twisted American Family Association headed by that idiot, Donald Wildmon. Now, as I'm sure everyone of you reading this compilation know, Donny has been spinning like a psychotic top in the name of enforcing his individual moral standards on the rest of us stupid clods. A few of Wildmon's rabid followers decided to bully and threaten these two women, resulting in Shannon going into hiding out of fear for her family, shortly after one of these tobacco-chewing slugs threatened her via sending a death threat home in her elementary-school-age daughter's notebook. During this time, Joan Cissom died, leaving Shannon to fight the good fight alone.

SPWAO came to her aid immediately, devoting the entire July/August 1990 newsletter to her plight. Looking back, I feel this was the most noble thing I have ever witnessed, and I was extremely proud to be a part of Shannon's support group.

Unfortunately, after receiving personally and reading publicly a myriad of letters such as the one I received from Linda Broggi, Shannon withdrew from the organization. After all, she wanted only to publish a magazine with horror stories. I have lost contact with her, but whenever I think of the rotten motherfuckers who are still trying to tell me what books I can write and read, what movies I can watch and own, I think of her and hope she is doing well.

Preceding my final column for the SPWAO newsletter is the piece I contributed to her defense. The final column addresses the letter by Linda Broggi, who claims she is a writer. I really don't give a fuck how she's doing these days.

My feelings as I penned this last column were a co-mingling of elation and sadness. I had taken the project full-circle and, in so doing, my viewpoint and skills at expressing this viewpoint had matured. I also realized the achievement of my initial goal: Everyone who saw fit to spend a portion of their life writing a letter, pro or con, to my column had been touched, more, they had been made to think about their position on the issues.

Think.

It was all I ever wanted and more than I ever expected.

AN OPEN LETTER TO THE CHAMBER OF COMMERCE, RIPLEY, MS

As a writer of Dark Fantasy, I am usually drawn to those circumstances which permit me to experience the bizarre and frightening side of human nature. However, I also live by the philosophy that I only write the stuff — I don't want to live it. It is for this reason that I will never set foot in your county. I have discovered that one of my own dared to cross the line between individuality and blind conformity in the hope that she might enlighten and entertain those of us who wish to be enlightened and entertained. Sadly, I feel that the region of the United States she chose to do this in wants nothing to do with either state of being. However, I also learned that she has been harassed, threatened, and censored. Of course, it is easy for this to happen when the majority of citizens are filled with hateful bigotry and intolerance. It's easy to be a bully; quite another matter to stand up to those who can fight back. May I suggest a trip to Missouri? Here, we love our guns and country as much as you do, but with one important difference: We realize what the country stands for — an insignificant thing called Freedom. As we watch you battle Shannon Riley, we also watch you battle Freedom. And that really pisses us off.

COLUMN TWELVE
March 1991

Fasten your seat belts and let's storm around the block like bats out of hell one last time.

Linda Broggi's letter in the November/December newsletter regarding my piece in defense of Shannon Riley disturbed me for two reasons. One, she expended entirely too much energy and too many words to respond to the roughly 200-word note that I wrote in the July/August newsletter. Two, she missed the point entirely, either by ignorance of the issue, or on purpose. I sincerely hope it was on purpose. Ms. Broggi cited people like myself as a major reason for the problems in this country, i.e. dividing Americans into "us and them" groups. Well, sorry, Pollyanna, but you're in bad need of a wake-up call, because where censorship is concerned, it certainly is a case of us against them. I'm sorry you saw fit to pervert the issue by tying in the Civil Rights Movement, a completely irrelevant analogy. Should you have occasion to read a threatening note tucked away in your child's schoolbook (as Shannon did) because of what you have written, drawn, and distributed, look me up. I'm sure you'll be able to understand then that it is not a case of where you live, it's a case of people who are not content to merely agree or disagree on an intellectual level, but choose to employ terrorist tactics on persons whom they perceive can't fight back. I call it Bully Mentality and it does exist, stronger in some places than in others. Thanks for writing.

I got a neat letter from Mike Arnzen, our Director of Publication Dispersal, with an even neater question. I tried to avoid the entire issue, but let's talk about it for a second.

As you know, we are at war with the Middle East. (If you have family or friends serving there, please accept my well-wishes for a safe and speedy return home.) Mike was concerned about censorship in the media, and for good reason — it is alive and well in this context, in fact, I've seen the words *Cleared by So-and-So Censors* on CNN more times than I can count. But, this cannot be considered as creative censorship, which is what I've addressed for two years. It is, simply put, a case of keeping military strategy on both sides a heavily-guarded secret. The equation of war at the bottom line is almost juvenile: Both sides want to win. Since this war is the first in recorded history with the immediacy presented by CNN, there is naturally restrictions and errors in reporting. Therefore, be vigilant and, above all, be patient. Creativity is not at stake in that arena.

On the other hand, in *our* arena, creativity is very much at stake. You guys and gals consider these questions, formulate the answers, and then make the answers part of your personal philosophy. I've never left you hanging before, and I won't start now. My own answers are in the parentheses.

Are words, as presented verbally or printed on paper obscene? (No.)

Should pornography, as it applies to publications such as Playboy *and* Penthouse, *be removed from the shelves of public merchants?* (No.)

If a book, magazine, article, letter, movie, or spoken viewpoint is different from your own to the point of causing absolute disagreement and disgust to you, do you have the right to protest the offending example? (Yes.)

Do you have the right to remove said offending example from the public eye? (No.)

Do you think that if someone ran through a shopping mall naked while beating a child with one hand and masturbating with the other, that person should be arrested?

I won't give you to my answer to that one. If you've read the previous columns, you already know my response.

I've put off this last bit as long as I can — we're rounding the block and damn near done with the ride. But before you get out, listen to this.

Babies, I want you all to know that your letters, pro and anti-censorship, fueled this vehicle for two years. My message to the Pros is this: Thanks for writing. Nothing personal. My message to the Antis is this: Thanks for writing.

These cryptic messages mean one thing. This is the last installment of Censoring the Censors, and you've all graduated. No matter what your viewpoint was concerning each topic, I appreciated and learned from every letter I read in the newsletter and every letter I received at Darkmoor.

Unfortunately, the threat of censorship will not end with this column. Because this is one of the most important issues facing a creative artist, the forum will continue under the capable hands of Doni Lazenby. Rest assured that you'll be guaranteed the same hard-hitting presentation that I delivered. In fact, I wouldn't be surprised if Doni does it better, so look out. I ask one thing of those members who desire to write letters in response, good or bad, to my columns — send them directly to me. I'll answer all who enclose a SASE.

I leave you with this.

There's only one person who can tell you what you can create and that's *you*. Billy Joel says the same thing at the end of every one of his concerts — *Don't take no shit off anybody*.

And certainly, most definitely, not the Censors.

INTRODUCTION:
Life in the Censored Lane

This little tirade began as an installment to Censoring the Censors, but it ended up as a stand-alone essay written on-spec for *Gauntlet* magazine. If this was a self-help guide for writers, I would say something like, "Fellow enlightened Dudes and Dudettes, don't *ever* do an assignment on-spec", but since it isn't, hell I don't care. Go ahead and do one.

Although dated, the essay speaks to one of the major censorship issues of our day. It is published here for the first time.

LIFE IN THE CENSORED LANE

Although the phrase, *Hey, hey, my, my, Rock n' Roll will never die* from a song by Neil Young may hold true to many fans, the fact is that popular music is indeed in danger of dying. The current wave of protest from the Parents Music Resource Center (PMRC) is doing its best to insure just that.

The PMRC, founded by Tipper Gore, wife of Senator Al Gore, has grown from a small operation to several thousand rabid followers. Indeed, the bills offered for consideration assume that many persons exposed to the "offensive" lyrics found in the music of such diverse groups as *Guns N' Roses* and *John Cougar Mellencamp*, are driven to take drugs or to commit violent acts. Proposals from the PMRC and other legislators have run the gamut from merely labeling records with a parental advisory to requiring two versions of an album — one censored version for those under eighteen, another for adults, with the adult version available only upon request, as if it were an X-rated videocassette.

There have also been ludicrous ideas such as requirements for each retailer to label the albums on their own, after listening to them, which means that when you buy an album you think is new, it's really not, because it's been opened and played a least once for the purpose of affixing a sticker that says the lyric content may be offensive. The worst thing about all the legislation designed to restrict all music in general, rock music in particular, is that many of the people you believed in and voted for are paving the way for the freedom to purchase and listen to only what they think you should. And if you think you're doing your job against this wave of pure repression because you're a

Democrat or a Republican, you're wrong. Think about it. When was the last time you checked with your Senator or Congressman to see how they feel on this issue? Because this issue is not divided between the two parties, you may be surprised at the answer.

What is the answer? First, it is necessary to identify the actual problem. The bottom line is that certain lyrics in rock music can actually be harmful to impressionable listeners. So, a body of people joined together to fight this menace, with their ultimate goal being to make it so hard to generate sales of the offending recording artists in the hope that they'll just fade away and leave these poor, impressionable people alone. And just who are these people in danger of becoming drooling criminal maniacs because they hear Guns N' Roses refer to heroin as a "real motherfucker" in their song *Mr. Brownstone*? Groups such as the PMRC would have you believe that it's the kid sacking your groceries and wearing a concert t-shirt. Not so. It's you and me. They're protecting us, these self-appointed moral guardians, from ourselves. They're also insuring that bad parents can continue to practice irresponsible methods of parenting while the Government acts as babysitter. After all, it's done in the Soviet Union, and it seems to be working there.

Webster's New World Dictionary defines a censor as "an official with the power to examine publications, movies, television programs, etc., and to remove or prohibit anything considered obscene, libelous, politically objectionable, etc."

Is that an elected position? It certainly sounds like one. Instead, we have bored Washington wives like Tipper Gore and Susan Baker who put their little heads together to come up with the PMRC. Now, it's grown into a monster that's scaring the hell out of record stores all over the country and getting results. Because they're worried about some kids smoking pot while they listen to this music and, since pot is illegal, it must mean only one thing — namely, that this music causes you to pursue illegal activities leading up to heinous crimes. Anyway, what would they know about it?

Plenty, if you believe Tipper's husband, Senator Al Gore, who admitted smoking pot in college last year when Reagan was in a frantic search to find a new Supreme Court Justice who wasn't a leftover 60's Head. What kind of music do you think Gore was listening to when he fired up that joint? The Mormon Tabernacle Choir? Chances are, however, that Gore was not listening to music, rather he was cruising around looking for gorgeous babes. Radical, man. Pass the Jack Daniels.

The simple fact is that music is just that. Some people are loyal to Country & Western, while others listen to only Jazz. Still more listen to a range of music, from Classical to Heavy Metal, but it's all for the same reason — music makes people feel good, it helps them get through the workday, it lifts them up after a bad day, it makes a party that much more of a success. It's a welcome companion during rush hour or a drive in the country. It can make you laugh or cry. But it cannot be blamed for indiscretions and crimes. Those, you have to take responsibility for yourself. After all, it's only music. A bad person will do bad things and try to blame anything around them except themselves everytime.

The artists aren't keeping silent during the furor, either. Many of them, notably Frank Zappa, who has raised two healthy children, is proposing that record stores keep a file of lyrics for each "questionable" album for consumer examination, but the opposing groups refuse to address this alternative as a viable solution to a problem they created in the first place. One must then assume that these groups, by their refusal to negotiate on their position, do not care to hear anything from the musicians because the musicians mean nothing to them. And that assumption is right on the money. They don't care about opinions from the people whom they attack, nor do they care about individual freedoms. What they care about is making personal decisions for people they will never meet. Decisions like the police would have made had they caught Al Gore smoking that joint.

Labeling albums serves one purpose and one purpose only: To exercise a need to flex the arm of someone in power, and that's a terrifying thing, because it starts with being able to put labels on records that fans will buy anyway, but it ends when that same small-minded individual garners enough power to stand before the ultimate button, smile brightly, and say "I'm pushing this because I can."

OVERVIEW

My involvement with the Small Press Writer's and Artist's Association lasted roughly five years. In that time, I met a lot of good people, a lot of Nervous-Nellies, a lot of uptight people who worried about what the mailman thought about them, and a lot of friends. From my emergence as new member to Censorship Columnist to finally, Treasurer, I came to understand that no matter what our differing ideologies were, everybody had one thing in common: They were creative people, whether the medium was the written word or the paintbrush.

These similarities despite the diverse membership proved to be the perfect gathering of people to entertain a forum on censorship. Those who agreed and disagreed with my viewpoints did so with a passion seldom seen in these days of diluted media information and mind-numbing obedience to the latest prime-time sitcoms.

I wasn't nice in my reporting of the events surrounding this issue — some even thought I was downright hateful and, in many cases, I was. It was beyond my restraint quotient as I told of people bullied and brutalized for publishing a magazine or selling a product to report these facts from behind the rose-colored glasses of naive apathy.

I had wondered long and hard what I would say in this Overview. At first, I thought of giving you yet another dose of Censoring the Censors, but then I reconsidered. After all, how could this issue be laid to rest with these final words? I realized that, unfortunately, censorship is never going to just disappear, as long as people are constantly auditioning for the role of their Brother's Keeper. There will be others, like myself, who rage at the darkness in their small way, still others, like Donald Wildmon, who will pervert the essence of Freedom in God's name, and still others like the majority of the SPWAO membership who will simply sit back and watch. The psychology of spectators is a strange one, indeed. We will rubberneck at a freeway accident, consciously or unconsciously hoping to see the gore of human tragedy, like watching a movie, a certain feeling that "this is not real" fogging our senses. We will read in the newspaper of a maniac who can't get a hard-on so he stalks the shopping mall parking lots, killing women, and we will feel the same vague, unreal terror we feel when we read a piece of fiction.

So it goes with censorship.

The trouble with the examples provided above is that they are almost impossible to avoid, surprise attacks from the world around us. Not so with a group that begins a campaign to restrict and destroy creative works and the ability to enjoy them. We usually have a loud warning, far in advance, of this kind of attack. *This* is when our inaction as spectators is just as great a crime as pre-meditated murder.

As a writer, I have forsaken a great deal of what others take for granted — instead of going out whenever I want to, I have to schedule and squeeze every gram of playtime into my daily routine. So, when someone says "So-and-So's Heavy Metal music is the work of the Devil" and they succeed in removing it from my local record store, they've also succeeded in destroying precious few free minutes I could've spent listening to that music. You think that doesn't piss me off? At least enough to speak out against those bastards? And, listen to me and listen hard, that tired, sack of shit argument about the Youth of America being ruined by this stuff has no validity whatsoever. As an American adult, I demand my right to listen to or read whatever creative offering I choose to! This demand is called exercising the First Amendment and it was created by people who not only believed in Freedom, they insisted on it after coming from a country where they had been denied this basic human right for so long. They, like many of us, were/are sick and tired of assholes telling them/us how to walk, talk, and think.

Since Censoring the Censors, many more incidents have occurred, and many more will undoubtedly occur in the near and far future. To attempt to encapsulate them all would be ludicrous and, as those of you who followed my column know, I was never ludicrous. Out of control, maybe, but never ludicrous. Thus, I'm giving you a final, personal philosophy that was born of and matured from the column in the SPWAO newsletter entitled *Censoring the Censors*.

If someone tells you that God hates a certain book or certain piece of music or certain movie, make them prove it. They cannot. If a Senate subcommittee votes against what you think after you've made your voice heard, then you vote those cocksuckers right out of office. If your home state Congressman says that a creative work is obscene and tries to push a Constitutional amendment to ban it, which is not what the Constitution is about, then you threaten the fucker with a minimum-wage job unless he listens to the will of the people and not some special interest group. And if you don't like me using the word "fuck", then fuck you. Nobody forced you to read this, right?

Throughout 1989 and into 1991, I learned how to write a column, how to answer letters, and how to formulate an educated opinion and present it with a dash of humor and intensity. But most of all, I learned that people are being hurt in all sorts of ways by the torture we are putting our First Amendment rights through. It starts in the Small Press and spreads to the major publishing houses, festers in the film projects of college students and erupts in a geyser of infected pus through the big Hollywood production companies, splattering onto the wide screen in your local multi-cinema. Freedom sneezes in rural elementary schools whenever we ban a children's fairy tale, and full-blown pneumonia results when we remove books from University bookstores in cities. And Freedom goes into a coma when we sign a death warrant on an Author who dares write down what his conscience dictates.

I could go on and on, forever and ever, but I won't, because you and I have better, and hopefully grander things to do.

In two years, what did I learn as well as attempt to teach?

Censorship has no place in the United States.

Steve Beai, Farmersburg, IN, 1997